Praise for *The Flirta*
Ghazal el-B

'Sara M Saleh is a powerful and evocative voice in Australian literature. Her prose is stunning, aesthetic, simply gorgeous, and now, in *The Flirtation of Girls / Ghazal el-Banat*, we get to experience her truly unforgettable poetic side ... It is a powerful collection and will reverberate for years to come.' ***The Australian***

'Sara M Saleh writes of grief, migration, celebration and intimacy with embodied incantation. In just 100 pages, *The Flirtation of Girls* spins together the countless granules that make the Arab Australian identity so intricate.' ***The Big Issue***

'Thrums with the graciousness of community and solidarity, survival and resistance ... Saleh's voice is unyielding in its scrutiny and enticing in its lyricism.' ***ArtsHub***

'An enchanting read ... Saleh has perfected the art of depicting the Arab world and its people, both in the homeland and diaspora, with all its complexities, in a way that I think would make the great Palestinian poet forefather Darwish proud. *The Flirtation of Girls / Ghazal el-Banat* cements Saleh as an up-and-coming poet to watch.' ***Books+Publishing***

'I felt this beautiful and haunting poetry collection by Sydney poet, human rights activist and lawyer Sara M Saleh deep in my chest, with its themes of occupation, colonialism and defiance.' ***Pedestrian***

 Sara M Saleh is a writer/poet, human rights lawyer, and the daughter of Palestinian, Lebanese and Egyptian migrants. Her poems, essays and short stories have been published widely and she is co-editor of the ground-breaking 2019 anthology *Arab, Australian, Other: Stories on Race and Identity*. Her first novel is *Songs for the Dead and the Living* (Affirm Press, 2023). Her first poetry collection is *The Flirtation of Girls/Ghazal el-Banat* (UQP, 2023).

Sara is the first and only poet to win both the 2021 Peter Porter Poetry Prize and the 2020 Judith Wright Poetry Prize. She is the recipient of the inaugural Affirm fellowship for Sweatshop writers, a Neilma Sidney travel grant, Varuna writers residency, and Amant writers residency in Brooklyn, New York, amongst other honours.

Sara is based on Bidjigal land with her partner and their cats, Cappy and Lola.

The Flirtation of Girls

Ghazal El-Banat

Sara M Saleh

First published 2023 by University of Queensland Press
PO Box 6042, St Lucia, Queensland 4067 Australia
Reprinted 2024

University of Queensland Press (UQP) acknowledges the Traditional Owners and
their custodianship of the lands on which UQP operates. We pay our respects
to their Ancestors and their descendants, who continue cultural and spiritual
connections to Country. We recognise their valuable contributions to Australian
and global society.

uqp.com.au
reception@uqp.com.au

Cover design by Josh Durham
Cover art by Natasha Simonian (WhyNatt)
Author photograph by Stefanie Zingsheim
Typeset in 11.5/14 pt Adobe Garamond Pro by Post Pre-press Group, Brisbane
Printed in Australia by McPherson's Printing Group

  University of Queensland Press is assisted
by the Australian Government through
the Australia Council, its arts funding
and advisory body.

A catalogue record for this book is available from the National Library of Australia.

ISBN 978 0 7022 6628 7 (pbk)
ISBN 978 0 7022 6815 1 (epdf)

University of Queensland Press uses papers that are natural, renewable and
recyclable products made from wood grown in well-managed forests and other
controlled sources. The logging and manufacturing processes conform to the
environmental regulations of the country of origin.

To the Auntydotes

CONTENTS

girls who live forever

Self-cartography

I never knew
anything but an achromatic existence,
the titillations of a liberated life,
lassoed around – twisting, tightening,
never quite nailing the target.
If rope clasps and concedes,
more noose than halo, I imagine
whatever mettle is in me –
flits out like a shapeless silhouette,
fray by fray; yet the world does not tilt.

I pluck the rays of
a sickle moon.
I, the penumbra.
A wind unbound,
the iambics of maps rattling
and restraining.
There is many a casualty
when sharpening image to word,
the frontiers of every high,
accountable for my crimes.

Propulsions of my blunted breath,
the glow of me pulses, an arabesque of
desire: waves of wild strawberries,
ruches of dahlias. I glisten like the mildew
of grass clippings.

The days still banishing, refusing to do
my bidding. Hunger still hinged
in my hipbones.
I recognise that conquering, all that is
caustic.
I submerge into the cosmic
– my flaws outlast the summer.

forgotten girls

broken ghazal for broken door

At the mouth of your teta's bayt is a door,
the only way in a single key made for that door.

The key is with the Ghost/Gatekeeper.
The Ghost/Gatekeeper asks you, *Why now? Why this door?*

You want to say inside you is a long line of abandoned
daughters, a swarm of fleas, and a hunger for this door;

inside your hunger a rage to scorch this colony's fantasy. Instead
you say nothing. To find yourself is to become more door.

And what is the difference between silence
and truth but a surrender, and this door?

The floors keep shifting.
On the first: the blueprints for salvation.
On the second: the languaging of history.
The third: the naming of things.
Don't let them confuse you, you never meant
to mistake eternal punishment for a moment of divine
ecstasy. You searched for love and found carnage,
its fleshy interior. Stand there as long as you can,
guarded by bayt.
Even though you know,
they may never let you in through that door.

Aubade for the Ancestors

The setting: family home, wherever that may be
The characters: the Ancestors
The scene: the past

Hours earlier, the Bedouin woman said, *We cast spells on girls who don't want to get married.* She and Teta share a breath, hennaed hands cableknit together. *Sprinkle some salt to keep the evil gazes away,* her voice staticky with seeing too much. All the aunties talk over each other and decide: Teta will be thrown, headfirst, into the rabid hunger of dogs.

**

I can't imagine it, a girl that young. Teta, round-bellied and cross-legged on the scratchy carpet, ashy index finger flags across her. It traces prophecy in the coffee grooves of the finjan. *No one can bring back the dead. You know what's coming.* The soothsayer's words trapped in the tunnels of Teta's ears.

**

The night is shredded with bullets. *Now – is the time to run. Run!,* the radio chokes. By now the women are intimate with war. They sit with it. Joke with it. Have one hundred nicknames for it. They are steadfast in curiosity. Even when they don't have permission to enjoy things that belong to the men.

**

Our beloved will get sicker and sicker. The marrow of the land confuses cobwebs and thorns for its children. The war is lost, and the living just out of reach. The men came with the fire, its gold leaked over the city. Burnt women: deer stunned with dying. The men never like when women speak back to the archives. Country and how we became it.

**

Soon Teta will be older than the state.

The scene: the present

We bury Teta.
**

In the absence of inheritance, no paraphernalia or pomp,
I spoon black seed and honey into my mouth.
It doesn't cure anything, but it gives me something to do.
Pain keeps travelling through lineage until one of us is ready to feel it.
I incantation a third time, blow a knot and cover my palms across
the bookends of my shoulders.
**

You're more bomb fragment than daughter.
I stand in a bucket and drip-drip blessed water from a little glass
  test tube
Mama gave me two years ago, willing it to clear this chest, and all
    that cramps it.
That's what Mama said they did 'back in her day',
'back home', when they didn't mercocrome every ailment.
**

Some maladies cannot be cured with mercocrome and olive oil and
black seed and blessed water.
**

At least I can pop in two capsules of 'numb everything'.
There is nothing strong enough for when it visits …
I can't imagine it, aren't I too young? They didn't call it trauma then.
I don't call it that now.

/ end scene

The Year That Changed Everything

1948 is crooked, is chasm of the
century, is promised land – 'milk and
honey', find fruit in its foraging, a frenzy of
dust storms, sift through its sands, view it
shimmering silken through your windscreen

1948 is the Mediterranean and its charred
sky, is the queerest city on this planet,
is music full blast, dizzying fun-park ride,
is ancient ancient, don't you want to be
free in this future utopia, parade down the
streets, swaddled in your brightest rainbows

1948 is stockpile of prickly pears and the
poisonous eucalypts pleated across the vistas,
and we, invasive species, a sting of
wind passing in their flourishing,
an exit wound stitched up expertly

No outcry for that, no outcry still,
the land will come for you, I think it already
has, didn't they mention, there are bounties and
there is bounty and we have already paid dearly,
you stayed to be citizened, to be bronzed baby,
didn't they tell you this is your God-given right,
your inheritance, I should know, there is never
a good time to lose a country

City/Sitti of Grief

To Watani.

To my faltering.

The figs that fall here, untethered to the reddened sun

their blemished skin I peel and peel

their teaching and I learn nothing

the brink that took us away from you, there is always a brink

the jasmine bushes in the rear-view mirror

the roaming of your lap, palms pressed sweaty traps

the sifting and I find nothing

these streets I walk that do not know you

the way the rich gorge on the world

the leaving that was your last indignity

the agent at the airport who put our father in a locked room,
    made him beg

the breaking-news banner on the TV announcing we cannot
    return home

the nation that will not be home

the balcony shutters keeping out the night and all its creatures

the realisation that I will only be free when I want nothing

Insan is Arabic for human, its root N-A-SA – which is to forget, so to be human is to forget

the forgetting of the past so that country may survive us/may survive itself

the past and its grudges in the knots of our back

the language that is trapped in itself

this city, city of desperation, city of grief, city of AK-47

the expectation that someone like me only knows of death and bombs and

trauma and war and bombs and bombs and bombs

Fi Mahattet Masr

They told me to prepare my body for war
and I thought of my family.
The station is blistering with people on
their way to balmy Alexandrian shores –
their deep-seated secrets suspended in time like syrup.
I think of Herodotus and if 2500 years later,
he'd still call this place a gift.
Then I think of you.
I think of you and the Sinai, the story
of your beloved Musa and his revelations
in the oldest monastery in the world.
I think of the Suez, blessed portal, portend.
You called us ships sailing past each other
in lonely sea waters, desperate foghorns
drawn by the dawn's solitude,
the only affirmation of our existence –
the edge of the world nowhere in sight.
I think of your eyes, the colour of slate,
how they follow and follow my every move,
the edge of my body nowhere in sight.
I think of your baritone when you speak my name,
the syllables collapse into a crater across the deck.
I think of how certain bodies don't know that they're dead:
the marigolds we watered in Marsa Matruh, the hibiscus tea we sipped
in Heliopolis, the slums of the necropolis where the Sufi saints and the
despaired meet, beds by burial catacombs, my uterus.
The bleeding between my legs comes,
    and I know it as treason.

I think of first look between mother and newborn:
the difference between a life of heaven
and a life of hell. Nobody ever thinks of mothers.
What the Greek gods tell of their immortality,
I believe about loneliness.

You, an Effigy

You will find yourself on the corner of the street.
Pretend your life is about to get better.
You'll finally be touched in a way you've never been.
You might even get a good night's slee—

No, that's probably unlikely.

You walk past parks with playgrounds and yellowing trees,
a local church, a chicken shop. Even with its shabby buildings
and closed shutters, schools that don't stay open, pubs that do,
this town is sterile, unlike the chaos of Cairo and Beirut –
they're more city than any of us ever asked for –
this town is monotonous, and perhaps monotonous is
what you nee—

Could there be a future here?

Never mind, you'll never have it
until the homes inside you die but
the Mediterranean's Raouche and the Nile's Corniche
slide salty sweat down your back,
you can't outrun their waters or their wars.
And it's obvious that none of
your countries have ever been sorry.
And you are not the fucking prob—

So what if you are?

You always bought your own lies. They wanted you muted
    so you trilled,
they wanted you docile so you smoked and sang and danced
    in your lacy underwear.
For a while your days shimmered like dollar-store rhinestones,
but take a second look, and it's easy to catch what those men did to
    yo—

Isn't this your life now?

You're a bonfire running out of wood.
It's up to you. That awaited touch an intruder on your skin.
Isn't this loss so official. And you, so eager you won't ask questions.
You want to make a home of something without apologising for it.
But who will hold you in the middle of the civil war? Nobody told you
the cost of entering was losing your way back.

little city

little city, on your scorched days Rania and I pool our
khamsmiyehs,
buy Bonjus from baqqal abu Fadi, sell them for triple the price,
    'dollar law samaht',
this country has us believing we are so clever, so entrepreneurial,
the neighbourhood kids should be grateful,
'Khalto, look at us, don't we make you
proud?'

little city, on your anxious nights we gather in
balconies, lighthouse beacons with little-to-no
light, wreathed in smoke, we wait,
we sit, we speak, we speak over each
other, 'Ya 'alayeh inshaAllah', no one
actually wants to hear the answers,
I can't afford to trust the morning,
I am still learning to believe it when it
comes.

little city, we want to sing, want to giggle silly over
boys and simple things, but you have different
plans, young men on tanks cuss loudly,
young men on tanks whistle at us, eyes open
empty, this dark, this shatter,
we tell them we have God, but
I don't think they believe
us.

little city, we climb to the top of the steeple
stairs, quiet and quieter, past jasmine
bushes, past bullet holes, confetti
of '86, no one bothers with
plaster, is it any wonder we don't have
mothers and fathers, how long will you
hate yourself into something we can
love?

little city, trying to forget.

little city, how did you survive,
what did they call you ...

before Syria, before Israel, before France, before
Ottoman ...
before, before ...

little city, what becomes of history
if there remain no artists to write of it?

your pages are long, your patience
longer.

Recipe for dinner and destruction

You put it on the pot & someone leaps off a balcony & you
turn up the heat, for the cinnamon sticks to seep & call for
Maria & it's not her name but what your barren mouth can
pronounce & two maids before her Lakshani came in her
saree – she was made small by this country.
You hear the banks have fallen today & nothing is going
right & you starve Maria, send her to her room & you let
the stew simmer, flavours in hiding & your curse words trim
the air & seize her passports, hold her hostage. Coriander
seeds greet comrades & you're decent, Maria should be
grateful, at least you hadn't left her homeless during the
pandemic.
The steam is fragrant & you think of the lives piled up
in Baabda and Jal El Dib, they are somebody's mother,
daughter, sister, as you sprinkle allspice & the cloves crack
& the last girl refused to remove the glint of gold in her nose
& you got rid of her when your nineteen-year-old boy snuck
his way inside her & you ignored the screams, they sounded
like broken piano keys.
& it's their fault, they want too much, 'but at least my
Filipina is cleaner than the Sri Lankan',
your friends say. Nepalese, Bangladeshi, and Ethiopian,
too – the difference between mercy and justice is how you
repent.
& kafala and kafara are only one letter apart.

Abolish the kafala system

Ode to Garbage (akh ya Libnen)

We say, *basita*, just sidestep the garbage piling up on the sidewalks of Verdun and Hamra

The power goes off and all the bakeries and the butchers stop

We say, *ijit el kahraba*, what we mean is, check everything in the fridge

We can't afford to call each other, we say, *3mele missed*

Our taxis are Mercedes – crumbling, holes in the floor

It's never, *I'm late*, it's *fee 3aj2a* – at least the children are there to sell you cigarettes and tissues while you wait in clogged backstreets

Buffer zones and green lines mean blowing up water supplies your electricity your hospitals your schools your highways and byways

Ramlet el-Baida beach, the only public beach in the city, covered in battered lampposts and broken needles and decomposing foods – but at least there were also iridescent jellyfish, half-moons strewn across the shore, and shabby palm-frond cabanas. The closest thing to Eden

Bougainvillea gardens and guerrillas in our balconies as the rich filter the fighting out at Saint-George Sailing Club or Faraya Ski Resort

Every religion sells you its own version. In every one, God leads you on

Taif Accords mean absolution, no accountability for the years of atrocities

Old warlords are the new government, trade in your AKs and military uniforms for business suits and pocket squares

Old Syrian tanks are still stationed, twenty years after they got out – 'in case'

The Raouche rocks watch on from afar, while this country dissolves under its own weight

Another fundraiser, another NGO worker, another journalist dancing and drinking the violence away in Gemmayze. We'll be another racist *New York Times* headline tomorrow

Beirut is a graveyard: havens and retreats reconstructed over weapons and mass graves

Sewer drains overflow onto the streets and private shame becomes public spectacle and a sewage-smelling sea goes up into the heavens and rains back on us, a collective punishment for our neglect

Akh ya libnen – it's never good news when I've heard that said

b ekher m3ammar Allah – the ends of what God created, but you already chose your part in the end, ya libnen

Reading Darwish at Qalandia Checkpoint

How long have you been waiting?
I just got here.

How long have you been waiting?
A few hours.

How long have you been waiting?
All night.

How long have you been waiting?
Since the day I was born.

A woman is standing too close behind me in this
swollen crowd, her breath foggy on my neck.

I thumb the pages of my book
and sigh loudly. She sighs back.

And I can feel all the ghosts through
the towers of barbed wire and cameras:

The baba holding his clothes up like a flag
at the guards behind the tinted glass.

The law student eager to make it to the final exam,
her messy bun pinned in place with a 2B pencil.

The teta, ready since the rooster sang sunrise
in, with her permit to begin chemotherapy.

The devoted husband on his wedding day; he doesn't know
in a few hours his body will be a bargaining chip.

The young man with autism who they will chase and
shoot at his school gates. Police investigation pending.

And I think of Cassius Turvey, fifteen-year-old Indigenous boy
who was punched and stabbed for being Black.

Palestinians know about going to school
and not making it back.

No resolution, no report, no textbook stops
this.

Police investigation still pending.

~~The evidence~~ – REDACTED
~~His rights~~ – REDACTED
~~His childhood~~ – REDACTED

No conventions, no condemnations save him.

At Qalandia, the soldier cradles his Uzi comfortingly,
like an instrument he is performing,
the olive branch insignia on his uniform flashes
in the haze of lights and multilingual
greetings signs behind him.

The soldier greets his comrade hello,
revealing teeth that match their belts of
ammo. They talk about the settlements that are
expanding.
'Thank God for cheap social housing.'

We find ways to survive this daily exercise
in humiliation, to numb the abyss of time. Each
moment any of us remains alive is a miracle.

I flip through the pages of
my book. Reading Darwish at Qalandia
is a provocation.
I confront the bare iron grids,
they are bone waiting for skin,
the toothed bars not wide enough
to squeeze a single orange in.

Min hala2 la wein?
after Etel

To all the lives lost in the Beirut Blast, 4 August 2020.

To wake up. To wipe the slumber from your eyes.
To read a single message. To re-read. To sit, to straighten up, to stand, to shudder.
To call and the dial tone beeps tauntingly, to swipe redial, to make sure.
To wait for a call. To check for calls. To check the group chats.
To check for more messages. For voice notes. To keep checking.
To scroll. To watch a video, silent, subtitles only. To scroll, to stop scrolling. To screen locking. Three seconds pass. To unlock screen, to scroll again.

To pace and pace. To stop pacing. To sit. To stand. To sit back down.
To check the time, the 2am luminous. To stomach grumbling.
To walk to the door, to pause, to exhale, to exit, to keep the door open this time.
To enter the kitchen, to fumble, to turn on the light, to squint, to falter.
To reach for the mug, to caress its chip, to put it down, to think about purchasing a new mug, maybe a whole set of them.
To dismiss the thought. To taste the mouth's staleness, teeth furry, to refuse to brush them.

To stare at the kettle. It stares back anticipating. To turn it on.
To rest on the counter, cool and smooth as pebble, to open the tea box, to select the tea, to decide on another, to rip the bag, to release its loose leaves, to pour the boiling water, to drip, to stir and stir, to inhale the steam. To blow, to sip, to sting your tongue, to keep sipping, the tea swimming in your cheeks. To slosh, to spill, to leave the spillage. To stare out the window, to notice the garden's weeds,

to forget the garden's weeds. To wonder what else is out there, what aliens, what jinn, the amorphousness, the blur of human and hidden.

To hear a siren, to flick a light switch on, to flick them all on. To pick at a scab, to scratch the crust. To unlock the phone, to tap into the family group chat, then another. To watch more videos, to read platitudes, to find the platitudes all trite. To slouch, to linger, to trudge down the hallway and back. To question how long the night is. To recite al-Muawathat. To finally reach her. To know she is safe but not okay. To console, to comfort, to resort to platitudes. To love and hate Beirut. To love and hate her people, her politicians. To question the necessity of humanity. To blame and blame and blame. To swear. To stop speaking. To recall that still, nothing seems to have changed. To pretend all will be fine in the end, inshaAllah. To cry, to silence the crying, to disregard the tears, to sniff, to wipe the snot with the right sleeve. To want to rest, to reawaken the dead, to see history repeat itself, to promise to do better, to know that most of this world won't do better.

Live from Gaza

funeral these headlines

                their insidious &

        the facts

        the theatricality of chaos

our lands

our traumas

        right to self-defence

        until 'complete quiet'

yesterday &

today &

tomorrow

report the stories of

            siren

        shelter

        monster

mayhem

&

death toll

the bias of those

under bombardment

the false equivalence
the certainty

in script

&

circumstance
in distortion

in the twitch and spasm
the absolute ~~lie~~ loss

telling
the truth

&

power
of

the narrative

the may/be in the testimony
the complicated in the detail
the question in alleged
the myth in question

existence

is
assault
is
escalation
is
conflict
is
dozens killed
is
air strikes

investigation

is
children
is
shield
is
the militants
is
schools

is
sides

Gaza

is
retaliation
is
the buildings
is
humanitarian crisis
is
strip
is
ceasefire

freedom

is
sand
is
world
is
cage
is
murder
is
ours

existence is

assault is
escalation is
conflict is
dozens killed is
air strikes is
investigation is
children is
shield is
the militants is
schools is
sides is
Gaza is
retaliation is
the buildings is
humanitarian crisis is
strip is
ceasefire is
freedom is
sand is
world is
cage is
murder is
ours was

In memory of

In memory of Baraa al-Gharabli
In memory of Mustafa Obaid
In memory of Yazan al-Masri
In memory of Marwan al-Masri
In memory of Rahaf al-Masri
In memory of Ibrahim al-Masri
In memory of Hamada al-Emour
In memory of Ammar al-Emour
In memory of Mahmoud Tolbeh
In memory of Yahya Khalifa
In memory of Fawziya Abu Faris
In memory of Muhammad-Zain al-Attar
In memory of Amira al-Attar
In memory of Islam al-Attar
In memory of Suheib al-Hadidi
In memory of Yahya al-Hadidi
In memory of Osama al-Hadidi
In memory of Abdurrahman al-Hadidi
In memory of Yara al-Qawlaq
In memory of Hala al-Qawlaq
In memory of Rula al-Qawlaq
In memory of Zaid al-Qawlaq
In memory of Qusai al-Qawlaq
In memory of Adam al-Qawlaq
In memory of Ahmad al-Qawlaq
In memory of Hana al-Qawlaq
In memory of Dima al-Ifranji
In memory of Yazan al-Ifranji
In memory of Mira al-Ifranji
In memory of Amir al-Ifranji

In memory of Dana Ishkontana
In memory of Lana Ishkontana
In memory of Yahya Ishkontana
In memory of Zain Ishkontana
In memory of Tala Abu Elouf
In memory of Tawfiq Abu Elouf
In memory of Rafeef Abu Dayer
In memory of Dima Asaliyah
In memory of
In memory of
In memory of
In memory of
In memory o
In memory
In memor
In memo
In mem
In me
In m
In
I

flirty girls

The (Not So) Secret Life of 3arab Girls: Our Raqs Is Sharqi (An Intermittent Ghazal)

after Patricia Smith

They can't stop us 3arab girls, spring coil curls, sentimental lines of kohl, hums, hollers and trills, *Allah, Allah, Allah,* dropping our raqs sharqi.

Stepping out in scarves and tassels, strong backs we strut and swing, on streets, at weddings, in living rooms, chest to chest, pot belly to pot belly.

The record skips, belt up them wide hips, henna night is vibin'. *Aweeeeha, glory be to our pure bride,* her teta ululates, *li li li.*

Drums thump, sweaty, stretch-marked thighs rub, shame at our feet, tonight I am not difficult to love, watch these sides shake and shimmy.

Gears whirring, grinding, blazing, *Ya banat, glide up that galabeya,* dip like Tahia, Samia and Hind, swerve those curves on that God-given body.

They can't stop us 3arab girls, dancing til fajr interrupts, swatting white 'belly dancers' in genie pants gyrating unceremoniously.

Mothers and daughters and sisters and beloveds, slide on over, and slide it good. Give thanks to the Divine as we revive the sacred raqs, raqs sharqi.

Kan ya Makan/Groppi

In the afternoon we buff our hair, foam roll
and steam it, mix hot caramel and sugar and
lemon on the stove, paint our toes, we tighten,
twirl, pout and pose. In polka dots and bows
and an allowance too scant for our dreams
and the metropolis that is made for them. To-
night our troubles adrift. We matinee at the Metro,
for a few crumpled-up pounds we sit
in the dark with Gregory and Clark. Hungry, we
head over to the centre of Tahrir Square, in all
its majesty, where Groppi sits like a sash, we
split a cassata, licking the jam juices on our tips,
over the vinyl, Abdel Wahab mawals and moans,
we shiver as the waiter 'am Samir tells us we're
mere metres from Azbakiya where
Umm Kulthum sang incomparable, incandescent.
At Groppi, we spot poets, actors, dancers –
golden age of cabaret and Tahiya
Carioca and the shoe she threw at an American.
At Groppi, cabs cross Qasr El Nil to drop off
eager families. Amal plays big sister, reassures
us we will have good futures. There
was, and there will be once more. For now,
at Groppi, we laugh, we complain about our
parents, and how we can't go back to Beirut. We
fall in love with the cute boy in the corner reading.
We stroll back home through the square
– of dreams and failed revolutions and revolutionaries.

Woman crying uncontrollably in the next stall responds

A response to Kim Addonizio

I have woken in my dress half off zip broken at 4am
have closed my legs to someone I loved they left
and opened them to someone I didn't thrashed restless
against 600 thread count soft and the glow of my mobile
phone the only light I saw for days cried miserable by the
sea confetti of condoms and spliffs chafing my ankles
one week's earnings got me a break-up haircut bangs
that didn't suit my round face backed away from the
mirror plotted all the ways I could kill him with my
friends forensic scientists and lawyers so we would get
away with it have bled into the back seat never used a
tampon – '*haram*', 'teen pregnancy' – have skinny-dipped
in a rockpool under the sky's drainage sung into a hairbrush
the pedestal fan an autotune hiked up a cliff to spot the
crescent moon feasted on the stars ripped out the stitches
with my bare hands because why not I thought nothing and
no one can / I hear you thank you for seeing me I want
to believe you when you say joy is coming.

Stone

To the first uninvited guest who
squeezed my chest
at the back of Ravi's grocery store
when I was eleven

your breath smells of
juicy biryani and sultanas
body heaving against mine
lick those rotting teeth
your eyes unwrap me
like candy
if I said no
you must not have
heard it
you hardened with desperation
for my plump
youth
my virginity
fastened to me
what do you dream of
as you greedily unpeel

you got off with
a minor warning
kept your job
this should not come
as a surprise
Medusa was assaulted
then punished for it
maybe we had it all
wrong
what if the writhing
mass of snakes
are men petrified
not for revenge
but justice
I am no one's victim
will not pay for being
someone else's sin

Tell me, what does it feel like
as I look you right in the eye –
slowly crush you from
the inside
turn you into stone

Ode to the WS train lines
aka 'Evil in the Suburbs'

T3

Today I am eyeing out this group of exotic white people
trespassing on The Area. Where we split $9 Thai and
teh tarik, where 200 languages molest each other on
the platform every morning. Where the best tailors sew
sleeves onto all my dresses, and where our love was busted
by the Ethnic Aunty News Network in the parking lot.
Where I don't need to translate the doctor's words to Baba.
Its streets a place I cannot hide from myself, home of the
halal snack packs, of hijabi influencers, beards and braided
chains and Nike TNs and FOBs and slam poets and
die-hard doggies fans.
A stage where I am seeing and seen. It never sleeps.

T5

Souped-up Subarus, the sheesha cafés, catcalls and bitchy
aunty commentary blot Station Street. Like hundreds of
confessions we make our way to the place of our worship,
Fairfield Stars Palace.
I (almost) indulge in the abundance of Lynx and stronghold
hairspray and glitter,
the money that is obnoxiously spent but also gifted.
The 400+ wedding guests – phosphoric stories all over this
tacky celebration. And it's ours.
A stage and I am not suspect.

This country tries to rid itself of us, as it has done to others
before – but we are still here. 350,000 and counting.

The Fever (Nights Like This)

after Nikky Finney

The hallway heaves with winter and I cradle my notes close
to my chest. I wonder why there are no trophy cases, no
photos with blazers, ties, milky smiles, no works of art –
'beautiful' or otherwise – on display. Only red buckets
breadcrumbed under a leaking ceiling. 'Don't worry if
they're a little rough – it's a rough neighbourhood,' the
receptionist shrugs, taking me up three flights of stairs.
I hold onto my poetry prompts like cheap souvenirs. Like a
bouquet of Luka Lesson and Omar Musa videos are enough
to alter an adolescence of after-school stop-and-searches
and midnight raids and military tanks and curfews – the
syllabus in Granville, Western Sydney.

I arrive at Mrs Hanan's classroom of unripened beards
and body odour and 'yeeeah, cuzzies!' 'Miss, where are
you from?' A foreign body in this place where there are no
distress signals or discernible marks to show the damage
of the last few decades in their homes, in their schools,
on their streets. Another classmate chased by five police
officers this week. They beat his God out of him, around
the corner from Ali's grocery and ol' man Türkiye's bakery
and the junction of the two rivers where Gadigal from the
east and western Dharug peoples meet, under a drapery
of stringybark, blackbutt and box trees. Power pulses
through here.

Here is Blaxcell and his avenue, local paper reporting gang
crime, illegal brothels, rundown shopping centre, sixty
languages tonguing each other, eviction notices, lines of

coke on collarbone. Here is the Lord Mayor of Parramatta
calling it 'the most urban decayed area in Sydney'. Power
pulses through these curious creative stubborn bodies.
Fever is a body fighting, is a body healing. It is elegy for the
disease of wanting. I am entering their world, incendiary
and cindered, twenty-one faces devouring alphabet,
sweat percolating onto their foreheads. They are like our
motherlands, in disarray. 'At least they can write about
Cronulla and Christchurch and shit,' a poet once said to me.
'I'm not that interesting now … I'm just White.'

I ask the Year 10s to share what they have written. I, too, am
coveting their gutturals and the cedar corseting their chests.
They pause, their kohled eyes autopsy me, returning the
favour. They are used to spectators. They are still deciding
if I am here to starve the fever or break it. One with a fresh
fade and chunky link chain, flipping a Zippo between his
fingers. Next to him, torn shirt pocket, mouth open like
a wet cave as he watches the clock. The room is soaked in
sunlight now and the soreness of the fever campaigning
to come out. Osama – 'but call me Sam' – has bullets
for cheeks. He deems me alright and recites his word
rosary, his brother locked up in Silverwater, his mother's
*hasbiyallah*s, his pride a torchlight moving through thick
fog. Temperature rises another degree, symptoms curdle
the citrus morning at Granville High. Abood lays bare his
notebook and begins, he is more than a burnable thing –
passport, picture, film, his jiddo's Sunday 'bar-bee-cuu'.

I am flushed. The tenderness of this Friday khutba draws the
students out like fireflies. They want love much more than
history. They run to their childhoods, all the (other) versions

of it, this is not
an almost   an attempt   an asterisked poem.
Those writers have stayed with me, urging me to surrender
to the fever on Nights that do not let me go. On Nights
just like this.

Bad Immigrant

Who adjusted the antenna to snag a signal for 200+ Arabic
channels you didn't pay for.

Who get sent home with a teacher's note about the smell of
Mama's packed lunch.

Who keep sewing kits in the blue butter-biscuit tin, your
first childhood betrayal.

Who save coupons for that special occasion – your cousin's
cousin's graduation.

Who all talk at the same time every dinner and gathering
and celebration.

Who live on two mortgages, three doors down from Teta
and Jiddo.

Who go weddings looking like the city at Christmas,
all bangles and bright colour.

Who haggle at the souks of Lebkemba.

Who coddle all the words, roll them and knead them and
give them pet names.

Who have the cleanest bums. (bidet = weapon of choice)

Who trade mansaf for mantu over the fence.

Who not understood by their parents. Who not understood by their children.

Who look like a store sign, *no Islamic here, no halal here.* Who look like *they stole our jobs.*

Who sound like the speech 'final solution' 2.0.

Who funeralled our sons even when they're not dead.

Who know military tanks and choppers over the basketball courts.

Who refuse border force, their lines and their detention centres.

Who pledge allegiance to Black history, Black country.

Who look like Mohammed Saleh who look like Mohamed Awad who look like Zaahir and Gamal and Mohidin and the cab driver uncle, the pharmacist, the tradie, the devoted husband, the target practice, the 'Fuck off Lebs', the gangs and riots.

Who begged to be White.

Who spectacled us. Why did we watch?

This poem has a mother wound ...

after Darius Simpson

... will you sermon it / will you jazz and jive it / swing and
salsa it / will you *ti-ra-ra* sing it away / snap it like the strings
of a oud / will you hang your anxieties up on it / tiptoe
around it / build it an altar of crystals / read its horoscope
and translate its rising / will you wrap it around you the
way the sun wears the morning / will you teach it / does it
have the range / will you shove a kebab in it / will you roll it,
dough it / sprinkle za'atar on it / serve it up as a snack / will
you lather it thick in labneh w zait zaytoun / in gasoline /
will you plunge it in the sink, with your silverware and fine
bone china / rub and scrub it good / will you sniff it off like
that line of ice on that stranger in the bar's belly / will you
slowly comb through it, disentangle every kink / will you get
that mean all over it / will you abandon it like every lover
you've ever had / will you keep it chaste like khutbas said /
will you wudu the boys out of our beds / will you gnaw it
to its knees / tame it / taunt it / will you zip it up into a body
bag / drag it halfway across this city / into the pulsing traffic /
will you graffiti the alleys and the lanes with it / scream it in
the void / spread it like a purpleish bruise across the sky / take
it to the place where you learned to keep leaving / the place
you cried with your whole body / where you drowned a few
times each day / so they can see you / so they can see you /
will it set you free / will you remember to heal it /
And what if I wrote the damn thing / in search of someone
to heal me

All the places my father lost his faith

my father lost his faith at the stale fringes of the brown
carpet in the apartment.
at his fifteen-hour shifts but always made it to bedtime,
tended to us with his tales of Sindbad the adventurer.

my father lost his faith at Camp David, at the cold peace,
at Abdel Nasser's pan-Arabism eroding.

my father lost his faith at my grandfather's goodbye,
begging us to go somewhere safer.
my father lost his faith during delayed take-off; he missed
my grandfather's death by an hour.

my father lost his faith in a country of men. he cried with
the love reserved for son when all he had were daughters.

my father lost his faith at the café, longing for the kind
of koshary black tea that bathes each rib.

my father lost his faith at his accent scratching its way out
of his multilingual throat:
at EFTOPS, at BORGAR, at HANDRED BERCENT.

at the rejection letters that came in the dozens,
at his degree he pulled out like a birthmark, a covenant,
an eleventh finger.
all the generations of men before him in the folds
of that paper.

my father lost his faith at my thirtieth birthday dinner,
red velvet and his leukaemia diagnosis delivered that day.
at the hospital where the nurse kept missing the vein,
his arteries recoiling with each tap.

my father lost his faith at the windowless rooms
resplendent rows of pokies calling. a culling of fathers
everywhere.

my father lost his faith when we lost the house – an
immigrant's downfall.
our last night in it, my father cried.
his cries little, lonely fires. they cling to me like a legacy.

I should have cut him in half, see what's eating at his rind,
what parting of seas sutured him together: his want for a life
of more.

I think I was terrified of seeing him then.
it would have been my first lesson in loving something
that stopped knowing how to love me in return.

Punctuation as Organised Violence

A response to Sun of Consciousness *and other works by Édouard Glissant*

—

1. Thirty years ago, my folks migrated to a city half dipped in ocean. To this day, they are sepia-faced and prayer-shaped, coal soot and cedar hills still rolling underneath their fingernails.

2. Arab-Australian
   Arab Australian
   ArabAustralian

   This arbiter of gods. This wretched frontier: duality or hybridity?

3. The Arabic language does not have hyphens, because the breaking of something from the inside is not allowed
   or we continue on as if it is not broken.

   We ration bags of za'atar and green almonds and joke in our parents' accents. In this place, we have learned to leaven like dough.

4. Colony wants to uproot the cedar from our nails. To be citizen is gauze negotiating with festering exit wound.

1. Father says. maybe it does not. always. have to be. a
   choice. between the smell of bread. or the smell of
   bullets.

2. The officer who watched the burning cities on my
   father's shoulders said, 'This land is for the living.
   For the free.' And stamped the papers. 'Welcome.
   Welcome.'
   Each welcome a blister. A pledge to an elusive
   'Australian future'.

3. Welcome. To back-beating labour. To being taxed out
   of beloved, grey-lipped houses, for the motorway and
   a multiplex centre. To brazen high-rises and rooftop
   gardens and high ceilings with delicate emerald
   trimmings. To where they constantly move salvation
   beyond our reach.

4. Application. Visa. Policy. Border. Fence. Ceremony.
   Father didn't know then, are all elements of fiction, too.

,

1. My folks grew me on a land thick with
   eucalyptus, moss, metropole, genocide

2. Arab, Australian, Other,
   Amen

   My first words stumbled out,
   shreds of language on a clumsy tongue,
   clenched in-between the aches of
   this suspect body

   our lands, our skies, our lines

   heirlooms
   cannot be fractured,
   or curated so quietly
   in your museums and galleries

3. Does a comma slow the chaos, or expand it?

4. Arab,
   Australian,
   Other

   In a drop-down list,
   who I am does not exist in English,
   violence
   enacted by a box,
   these algorithms
   of absence

’

1. Every day, Mama and Baba plant the alphabet at first light. Their citrus-skinned bodies are whole canons. Our lashes licking the sun, we make our way into the golden harvest.

2. Mama and Baba, they're so thin now. The words for what is killing us also thinning.

3. Apostrophe: to contract or to subdue; to possess

4. Sundays at Arabic school, we chewed mastic-flavoured gum loudly and rolled our eyes at Mr Hamza's conjugations. I must have missed the (grammar) lesson then: That which you think you possess first possesses you.

()

1. Australia
    Largest exports: metals, minerals, grains
    Largest imports: ~~machinery, precious metals, plastics,~~ human beings
    (Colony honours itself with statues and streets and medals and prefers we don't ask whose land we are on and who builds everything around here.)

2. The Migration Act (people are footnotes).

3. Colony is a chalk outline.

    We are up to our necks in fuel and muted prayers and neat piles of grief. Let us swing baseball bats instead of lighting more candles.
    I know it is not convenient (when will it be?)

4. Silence in a place is the same as not existing (and they expect us to not exist).

5. My folks did not march at protests and chant slogans and they never explained preferential voting. They lined up at the phone booth for hours as the promised rains came, cradling 50¢ coins and two screaming toddlers waiting for a chance to call home. They worked dishwashing and cleaning shifts to scrape enough for my medical bills and one book from the Scholastic sheet (and what is more revolutionary?)

CAPITAL

Invasion /
Terra Nullius /
White Australia /
Immigration /
English /
Multiculturalism /
Democracy /
Anti-Terror laws, over 82 and counting /
Countering Violent Extremism /
Afghanistan /
Iraq / / / / / / / / / / / / / / /

1. My people are not recognised in national legislation
    that protects from Racial Discrimination.
    Why do these Laws matter more than we do?
    (Do we matter at all?)
    What of these holy texts lodged deep in the dredges
    of country?

2. How long must we live in a world that only offers
    dust in our eyes and is there such a thing as courtesy
    in a War we never asked for?

3. I don't want a world where we are Almost Beautiful.

4. Is Death still any less Death if it is taking its time?

Border Control: Meditations

To my cities

*The questions two young soldiers asked me
at the King Hussein Bridge border crossing checkpoint ...*

Were you born on a Thursday in Cleopatra
Hospital? Did you come out silently, as day-
break smudged the night sky? And why was
your father absent? What is the name of your
father and his father and his father? Do your
neighbours Mohamed and Faduma water
the orphaned houseplant whenever you are
away? Are you aware your parents first arrived
in Australia with their life savings wrapped in
brown paper, their only English the lyrics to
'We Are the Champions'? Did your mother bring
two dresses, red polka dot and turquoise taffeta,
in her peeling '60s suitcase? Did you correct
her *thanks God*? Did she put up a fight when
you said you were leaving? When he left? And
how was your first Ramadan alone? Did you
miss the walnut ma3moul and *Allahu Akbar*s
tossed at you on Eid mornings? Have you told any-
one about the Enid Blyton books you stole from
Stanmore Library, because your mother worked
three jobs? If you flatten your gutturals is it still
Arabic? Why did your childhood best friend run
away? What man siphoned her dry? Why does
your grief stick to everything? Did inhaling an
onion help with the tear gas they threw during
the protests of '03? What remedies did you inherit

from your ancestors? What skeletons? Who taught
you to roll wara2 3enab like that? Does 2am still
grab you by the throat? Amongst the Gitanes and
sewage and Roman ruins, can Beirut forgive its
people? How many times have you phoned your
mother since? Does your grandmother always boil
her water twice? And why are you still shocked
at how things (don't) work there? What other
city turns its war bunkers into clubs? Its prayers
into curses? And why do the wretched always
sell roses on Bliss Street? And how do you revive
the dead? Why did they take your brother? Could
you make out his face amongst the thousands
flickering in the waters of the Mediterranean?
Did he return months after the funeral to ask
you, *What wrongs did I commit*? What village
do you carry on your lips, balance on your
breath? Have you been to Jerusalem during olive
harvest season? Did you pick and press, before the
settlers gathered like acid in your chest and
poisoned the ancient trees? Have you tired yet of
the *may Allah have mercy*s? Have they tired of
you? Were you afraid of the men with guns those
nights the power cut? Did you splutter your amens
and sweat out your tasabeeh? Do you remember
the countries you've lost? Do their crooked rivers
still cling to you? Did you hear the aunties, rusted
arms, coarse hairs on chins, call you lonely? Call
you nobody's mama anymore? Did you tell your
mama you named him Omar al-Farouq, after the
revered warrior? Why did it end with your Great Love
Who Changes Everything? Did he make your wide

hips tremble with jazz and derbake? Did he linger
long enough on each letter of *ya leil, ya ein* and
the evening news headlines? Did your hurts trail
behind him like tangled fishing lines, too much for
the life he lived? And does weight like that settle
or lift? And what of the days you feel the earth
greying? And when will you stop writing about borders
and bloodshed and war and death and home? and
home? and home?

Reading Darwish at the Museum of Falasteen

after Katie Hale

The air is fragranced with fresh semsem ka'ak
and jasmine and I am waiting for my mother.

I am forever running early, hopping on train after
train, always towards something. The museum

is fluorescent and cool, and the past is distilled
and maintained for us. I don't need a ticket

here, *welcome—it's free!* the smiling woman
at the front door says, she can see I haven't

been before. The tiled domes are handmade
and majestic, timeless as our ancestral lineage, shaped

in our image. There is simplicity, too, in the museum,
though the amount of calamity on display seems

deceptively complicated, and the ramp winds up
to floors and floors. From the peripheries, tour guides

rotate like planets, eager to assist, to tell of hero
and of villain. I am still adjusting to all our stories

made coherent, curated in a single structure. Sesame
seeds trail behind me like a dashed line on a map, but

there are cleaners to wipe up my mess. I am reading
Darwish in the café, where all the waitstaff are also

Palestinian, 'am Mohamed from Jenin, from Haifa, from
Beit Lahm, and all the guests are from everywhere, and

none of us ask why they suddenly care after all this
time. Perhaps they want to be part of history in

the present, where our people are displayed up on
walls and in cases and at the back of the exhibition.

The Purging

When you reconstruct my jaw
handle with sensitivity,
it is in ruin.

You'll find my mouth open for the first time in a while,
for so long it has been a citadel. An unholy well.
A wail will come out,
don't be surprised if you happen upon other noises in there, too,
my father's praise, prayers for Gaza
nesting in my throat.
You may also detect the perfect English, the Arabic subtitles my mouth
could never accommodate,
and the taste of tears, clementines and cardamom in the hinges …

Baptise this mouth of the screams
and the indignities when they came for us.
Cleanse it of the abstinence, the ghosts of wedding vows
that were never recited.

As you rebuild, the words
may appear in anarchy.
Please, purge them from my mouth.
I don't ever want to see them again.

There are no colonisers in this poem

Only worshippers at al-Aqsa breaking their fast / in i'tikāf all night /
the hakawati's stories flare through the Old City / in a crowd
of holiday wreaths and Christmas trees / which are trees and
not barbed wire / There are no colonisers in this poem / only
the old man / stringing and spiralling the cheesy knafeh / orange
blossom syrup caramelising his beard / another daughter returned
from exile / each arrival unclots his blood /
There are no colonisers in this poem / the snow
is unsentimental, the kids throw slush balls
at each other / there is no rush to get to class,
if they truant – it's their choice / they're just doing what
kids do / the ice-capped tourists / exit the Austrian Hospice /
hot chocolates warming their mittens / There are
no colonisers in this poem / only lovers in the back
of cars / slipping out of towns and villages with no farewell
or fanfare / for a lick of the big city and their lover's
lips / There are no colonisers in this poem / sparrows
release their breaths in rhapsody / commuters start their morning
shifts / or sleep-ins / they can expect to make it wherever /
There are no colonisers in this poem / water unsullied / clean
enough to quench gardens and groves / sons join their mothers
and fathers / and grandparents for dinner / and arguments are
just arguments and not manifestos / There are no colonisers
in this poem / there is only wild joy / we are all here /

Shireen would be too.

girls who live forever

Here, There: a Ghazal

To the people who came before us, who made themselves at home in the
tensions of these geographies so we might make our way beyond them.
— after Natalie Diaz

The barista in Chippendale wants to know where you're
from, mispronouncing your name,
a dismissal, an accusation, you are neither here nor there.

They came to your beloved Beirut and forced all the wrong
languages into your mouth,
you separated yourself into two piles of neither here nor there.

One night, before Taraweeh, Teta asks why you recite
Qur'an in cracks like that;
you drought your gutturals because you understand you are
from neither here nor there.

Your childhood was a series of Interruptions, every day a
kind of absence,
and you wonder can they love you if you are not enough,
here nor there?

You are orphaned from your mother/tongue, your longing
confused for every man you baptise lover,
and all the women in you are tired of running,
here and there.

To honour the questions, you must honour the answers,
only our poets have ways of teaching us that we are much
bigger than here and there.

Thistle [to lose a ~~lover/country~~]

Summer 2006

Yes, I kiss the boy who calls me soft
a kindness I can't forgive,
a forest of thistle surrounding us
a cover from the unbearable July heat
mounting in our breath.
Yes, I feign insouciance, try –
but under the patchwork of stratocumulus clouds
I can almost reach, the way light tethers itself to
darkness just to free it.

Yes, I followed you up the mountain, the furthest point,
this whole country is a three-hour road trip.
We are only days away from the bombing,
crossing the borders into Damascus. You to Cyprus.
The monsters will follow us the rest of our lives.

Yes, it's me, I try to be less monster.
I thought I could outrun the year I lost a country.
In a long line of many years, I lost many countries.
Yes, they destroyed my country
and I respond the only way I know how,
by letting them make a country of my body.
Yes, ever since I left I commemorate country into
combustible things – photographs, poetry, plastic film.
Mother, teach me how to unhold that boy
the way country unheld us.
I did not want to make myself open,

I did not want to make myself a poem.
Mother, teach me to flower like a thistle.
Teach me, teach me.

After the Apocalypse

... I look for anything to love

Blood-soaked sheets to signal my purity

Tracing the circumference of breasts, they blossom

The most beautiful part of my body is where he touches

7aram is a spectre I don't know how to disrobe

Did not know my body is a conquering and I'm in the crosshairs

The floods come in Arabic, the only language of loss left in the world

Seduced into the valleys between my fingers

Fajr trembles and I let him leave. This will be the last time,
we both lie

Kiss me the way one kisses a grenade before hurling it into the night

Like anything else can bleed this much and still call itself alive

Nafs is a lit match that will torch everything

Hundreds of ghosts sleep next to me

Why I keep emptying myself from something perfectly good

A Poetics of Forgetting

I.

I forget tradition, a tray of sticky dates passed around the
kitchen table, bismillah in our mouths before we ravenously
break the dusk, chew and spit back the pits. Ma ladling
lumpy lentil soup, abandonment pouched in her long sleeves,
an old injury she does not stop pressing. *How are we still
here?* Made of garlic breath, violent affection, arrears. Ma
pushes, *Alhamdullilah for these bounties, we are blessed, girls.*
These pleasantries,
these communal myths we tell to spare each other.

II.

I forget how I cannot see the stars, how the barbecued
smoke eats at the sky, how we elbow our way through
chattering heads congealed in every crack on Haldon. I
cannot see the sidewalk, but I hear it—*Sahlab! Sahlab!*
Mustachioed men in red tarbooshes summon us beneath
strings of plastic crescents—dangling babies shriek parents
into surrender—a siren wails somewhere. This evening
orchestra. My sisters dervish and droop: shiny baubles,
painted gold lids and hips, desires too big for the lives that
chose them. Ma says, *This love is haram*, so we learn to keep
our distance. *Together we remember the Lord.*
These celebrations,
these distractions we share to comfort one another.
And naming those who stray will not bring them back in
any religion.

III.

I forget how our Lebanon made its way to Lakemba.
Mothers of disappeared sons wait; they hold up headscarves
like white flags, like nooses; war wants us even in peacetime.
These Arab dogs, these ragheads, chalk outlines and choppers
crawling low. Our loss barely literate. We pretend not to
notice, this neighbourhood is an obituary.
These farewells,
these griefs we silence so we do not set ourselves on fire.

IV.

I forget how I awaken in the arms of another. How there are
no muezzins interrupting dawn, only this tango of breaths
and gasps. How I have dared to worship in a language that
is not Arabic, how I tried to scrub and scrub Ma's beauty
spots off my face. You are devoted to them, to this altar of
soft, turmeric skin and sadness. I shake the shame out of my
curls, I dip into the surge, the stagger, the rapture and the
rupture. The din—it ruined me, it split my god. I want to
pray, but I cannot recall the verses.
These divinations,
these transgressions, so I do not forget
every lonely night that ever was.

Elegy for a Body

How many fingers does it take, to do what
I never thought I would do to this body

Dust shelves, fold sheets, then shove a fist
back of the throat to bring order to my body

On Friday nights I don't sing 'Sawah', I hurtle towards
the Hate, this is the only way to accept this body

An unholy ritual and I am a stranger,
I cup the ashes, the impurities of somebody

I pull and pinch and stretch and scab
to be touched just enough by anybody

Page after page, I learn my Devil so I learn my God:
can either exist without the body?

Dr Diaz says, *The rot is deep, but you are not an
unspectacular thing*
Lover says, *I am tired of carrying this whole body*

Don't die, the ancestors say but they did not prepare
me for when I am the one to betray and call it body

All these years, I still don't know how
to say forgive me,
I am an elegy before I am a body

Palindrome for a good girl

Instructions

Lower your voice. Don't talk back. Be polite. Chew quietly.
Stay thin, don't eat that last bite. Do your chores. Always be
beautiful. Wax your moustache. Cut your nails, you're not a
lady of the night. Never reveal your age. Buy spare SPANX.
Maybe two. Bleach your black hair blonde. Pray. Know your
place, obey. Wear the lacy lingerie. Let him have his way. But
not too much – you can't be too easy.

My mother climbs into my body each morning,
a reminder I am not worthy.

In a toilet cubicle somewhere in Fez
I see shards of my reflection

in the tangerine tessellations.
I am ungathering.

But I can't stop putting things inside me.
I'm an irritation, an embarrassment, undesirable.

Isn't this the only way we can be disciplined?
When it's only me in the dark with my demons.

I pull back from the stall walls, from my image,
it's haram, the holy book instructs, to touch yourself.

Love poems are never for the girls who feel things.

Love poems are never for the girls who feel things.

It's haram, the holy book instructs, to touch yourself,
I pull back from the stall walls, from my image.

When it's only me in the dark with my demons,
isn't this the only way? We can be disciplined.

I'm an irritation, an embarrassment, undesirable,
but I can't stop putting things inside me.

I am ungathering.
In the tangerine tessellations,

I see shards of my reflection.
In a toilet cubicle somewhere in Fez,

a reminder: I am not worthy.
My mother climbs into my body each morning.

Progressive (White Lover)

after EvN

Shit.
I couldn't tell you what in the internalised Islamophobia
possessed me.
I just had to find myself
a White Lover.
Whose Twitter bio read ally.
Who posted a black tile.
Who likes his girls
copper-skinned, thicc thighs, hair unruly
I get the feeling I'm not the first one he's invaded.
That must make him an Authority on us.
Honey, he coos, *stop taking everything so seriously.*
Not everything is about race.
Because he listens to J*rdan P*terson
who said,
It's important to hear all sides equally.
Some sides are more equal than others.
Cancel culture is a cancer
stifles everyone in debate.
Some stifling is more equal than others.
White Lover is loud.
You have to admit,
there are some who rort the system.
Who don't accept the Australian way of life.
And what about those ISIS bros who hate women?
White Lover talks
and talks over me.
(*I'm too close to it, I'm not objective.*)

He doesn't want my brain,
only my acquiescent body.
He likes to argue with my jaded Muslim friends.
It's important to play devil's advocate.

The majority of victims of Islamophobia are women,
the news anchor declares,
fourfold increase in reported incidents after terrorist attack.

I tell myself this is the last time.
I will end things tomorrow
as White Lover walks through my front door.
One day it will be him
on the front page of *The Australian*:
Hysteria over white man who defends war criminals.

One day it will be him
we run out of town.

Eid 2016 (little and big)

A frost-tipped night in June

and Prime Minister offers his best wishes

to Muslims celebrating Eid al-Fitr.

Our 'leaders' invite ministers to

grand iftars and morning prayers.

I'd rather sit with the destitute.

Our 'leaders' also invite police.

Not a single imam or sheikh attend a BLM rally.

I'm three years away from sitting

on the edge of the masjid's front steps

where politicians will mourn.

Occam's razor.

This obscenity is where I re-enter.

Where are your hands, sluiced with

blood.

By Eid al-Adha, we know you are

waiting.

We know you are waiting

to take us to the slaughter.

Headlines

The first time we met, you asked me if I rode a camel to school

I hated myself

                              for laughing it off

The second time, why women weren't allowed to drive

After that,
                              it was

'caliphate cutie' / 'towelhead' / 'sand n*gger' / 'stone thrower'

                              on the bus, in class, at the movies

'they should sterilise you' / 'the only good Muslim is an ex-Muslim,
or a dead one' / 'don't blow yourself up'

                              in line at the post, online in posts,
                              every Halloween party

'ban the burqa' / 'ban the mosques' / 'ban halal'

                              in the papers, in parliament,
                              at the ballot box

Iraqi oil in Australian hands turns to wheat
burned rubber with a crisp mustard aftertaste.

We used to be sand n*ggers but
nowadays we're in the census, an ad on TV,
even a semi-decent character on *Grey's Anatomy* (well, a simulacrum
of one: she takes off the hijab – there's always something).

I really feel the mark of progress when I tick the check box
or what I call
fresh material for writing.

The End of the World

after Saeed Jones

*Dedicated to the victims of the Christchurch Terror Attack in
Al Noor Mosque, Allah yerhamhom.*

The End of the World was a mosque.
Brothers in freshly pressed white jilbabs, perfumed

necks, congregated in ceremony and symmetry,
tethered to each other on Friday afternoons. One

prostrating on the carpet, its emerald unequivocal as
the ocean he had crossed from Syria, next to him father

to first baby, hands up as sleep heavies his lids,
uncle in the wheelchair whose wife would try

to protect him. Look at that crowd every week, they were
ready to receive the truth in whichever shape it arrived.

The End of the World was thundering. Was bullet
ridden. Was still. Gunned down as they uttered

in devotion, Peace Be Upon Him. The End of the World
was refuge in the words, Allah Akbar, in the doors

always open despite the terrors,
this welcoming and wearying of us:
children dressing up for Eid,
the ginger cat lingering,

the women complaining
about the space. Alhamdullilah

for the sisters who couldn't make it that day.
As the white man stood at the gate
like a soldier, led by every other white
man who had brought him here to prey,
to massacre all the Muslims away.

Unholy Verses

How the seas emptied of salt
And the tides swelled
And the pipelines built
And the gas pumped
And the forests logged
And the fisheries depleted
And the reef bleached
And the mountains landslided
And the bees starved
And the stars absconded
And the sky broke open
And the planet tuberculated
And the corporations monetised
And the surveillance digitised
And the protestors fined
And the people calloused
And the laws ossified
And the women paid first
And the bodies of earth testified against us.

Lexicon

> The late Nizar Qabbani had once referred to Arabs
> obliged by distance and exile to write in languages
> not their own as wild horses. I took that to mean
> that he admired our freedom, but lamented our loss,
> perhaps even our unruliness …
>
> – Hisham Matar

To speak properly you need to learn
the difference between free and three.

She doesn't know what comes after,
so we begin again.

P not B
Repeat after me

But I can hear the B sound
billowing through the pillows of her cheeks
stained on her lips.

B for the beeps at the check-out counter
B for you're so beautiful, you'll make it here
B for be careful, it will get you into trouble.

P not B
Repeat after me
Vvvv not Fffff
palate cleanser.

Not Qa – Ka
Not Qa – Ka
kissing a fist.

And she rips the page,
paper shredding across
the kitchen table like live artillery
her hand the barrel of the gun.

Stay. She grabs the dustpan
brooms them like the melting
of a serpent's carcass,
deposits them in the trash.
Garbage bins really do hold our shame.

Again. An inflection,
her smile eating the inside of her mouth
dimples in her cheeks – like miniature moons.
I see the letters parachute onto the paper
floating quietly, like a breeze on its way,
I still hear it.
She's the one who teaches me to speak.

French Facelift

after Mohja Kahf

Let's break French open,
dissolve it into the golden sands of our deserts,
scrape it off our hardened tongues,
rub out its brazenness.

I'm going to make French more 3arabi,
drag it through the streets, beat and dust
it off like sheets on the clothesline,
relieve it of its Molière heritage, reassemble
its letters like the borders we inherited.

All our dialetics and languages from Ras Beirut
to the southernmost settlements of Madagascar
conspire together to ambush French, reverse its effects.

Let's give French a facelift:
henna its hands, infuse it with saffron and cinnamon
and sumac, streak its cheeks with plums and pomegranate
seeds, wrap it in a turban, douse it in Zam Zam.

French has never tasted anything as sweet
as clotted cream, rose water juices
dribbling across French pages, French poetry
French has never inhaled ground coffee this
celestial or written a ghazal reeling with tenderness.

French, with your 'romance', the audacity of your
silent letters and nasal vowels, I take your two gutturals
and raise you five.

Ode to Teta's Building

And the Aunties on the balcony and the ash in their lungs, titillating gossip on their tongues, the tubes coiled around their arms like rubber bangles And the unrelenting hand gestures And the bags of dried mint And the green shutters And the basket filled with fresh flatbread swinging from the rails And Dalida's sultry voice bruising the evening

Je suis malade …

And all the neighbourhood kids pile up like bricks And there's dabke and baladi and khaleeji in the driveway And scooters by the kerb, glass bottles and Bonjus boxes and Chiclets bubbles And the idioms And the coffee cup readings And the mops and brooms for a deep clean every time there is a spillage And the curtains drenched in permanent homemade smells of fried beans and onions and incense

Complement malade

And the electricity cuts <no more Dalida>

And the generator whirring, shuddering us on <*Someone press play on Dalida!*>

Comme quand ma mère sortait le soir

And the love affair he discovered when he walked into her room
And the crimson rags discarded when baby Mariam departed
And burglars climbing through the bedroom window
And you, smart enough to call out names of people
who weren't there

And shoes off – this building is communion
this building is an irrevocable condition

The day home didn't change

FIREFLIES

The beeping dial tone taunted me, like a handful of glass
scraping across my insides – it was a familiar feeling
following Lebanon's asphyxiating thirty-year civil war and
daily anxieties about what was happening and concern for
loved ones.
I had spent several hours trying to reach my mother in
Beirut after a massive explosion tore through the city's belly
that balmy summer evening of August 4th. In a desperate/
futile attempt to make sense of it, I watched, eyes puffed
like curdled milk, Instagram video after Twitter video
of destroyed homes, gutted cars, shattered windows. The
blast incinerated trees, rearranged the faces of centuries-old
buildings, pulled the ashen Mediterranean sealine inwards.
News outlets reported that the Beirut bomb was so huge it
was heard in Cyprus.

WHITENESS

During an event to fundraise for the victims of the Beirut
Blast, one of the speakers reminded the online audience that
our Home Affairs Minister once said resettling Lebanese
Muslims into Australia in the 1970s was a 'mistake'. A
statement one does not so readily forget, like a shadow that
momentarily shrinks in the corner as it prepares to grow
and swallow the whole room. Our discourse is bloated with
this type of Islamophobic, anti-Arab commentary, which is
regularly propagated by politicians in power (I write this as

we mark fifteen years since the Cronulla riots and almost two decades since 9/11).

In his seminal book *White Nation*, scholar Ghassan Hage argues that our various racialised identities in Australia are 'imagined, positioned, and managed as being in some way alien in relation to "Whiteness" and "White" values.' This is what Hage refers to as 'the fantasy of White supremacy', rooted in the identification with European empire, with conquest and colonisation.

'White' is the default Australian culture, and 'White people' imagine themselves as 'in control' of this default, of this version of Australia. This is an essential part of White Australia's imagination, a deliberate design to exclude, to induce feelings of exclusion – and to play on both. The more alien we feel, and are made to feel, the more displaced we become. The more displaced we are, the more eager many of us become to prove ourselves and our place here in this dominant version of Australia. Some through allegiance to this version and others to an alternative: to each other and to a 'like' community.

Diaspora

To fight this social, psychological dislocation, we invest in building Diaspora, where it can seem 'easier' to revive, maintain, or invent a unique interest and connection with a prior homeland – real or imagined, where there is no room or risk of forgetting, assimilating or distancing.

We reconstruct relics out of shared anxieties and feelings and rituals, rotate them on our spits. We take our drums and our derbake to the Opera House to protest 'our' Lebanese Government, find solace in the global family

WhatsApp group chats as we bond over multilingual memes and bizarre conspiracy theories and floral forwards, long for the ruins of Byblos and the shores of the Mediterranean bedazzled with silvery fish as we barbecue and hum along to Fairouz soundtrack on Sundays, gift each other containers of janarek in spring and frozen dried mint in autumn.

To exist in Diaspora is to exist within ambivalent, shifting fault lines, flamboyant and feeble. It is a continual conjugation of this hybridised Arab identity, faced with the double bind of racism and patriarchy as we ourselves perpetuate dispossession against the traditional custodians of this land.

Memory and myth

'One is always at home in one's past,' writes Vladimir Nabokov. Perhaps more accurately, we are at home in *the memory* of our past. A version of it. Ours and borrowed. And often the reality of this is a blurry picture of a past that can never be the present – or a past that never was.

We mourn past glories invoked by modern nationalism and liberation movements, and our inability to reclaim them – despite how many times we convince ourselves our beloved Lebanon will rise again. But country is a broken headstone.

The institutionalisation of memory and myth of our own resilience undoubtedly functions to help us cope – and in doing so, it is rather cruelly, ironically, a (reluctant) acquiescence of the conditions that made it necessary for us to rely on the idea in the first place. An acquiescence that has metastasised into intergenerational trauma, one of our few heirlooms as children of Diaspora.

PRIVILEGE

I have the privilege assigned by Diaspora, the privilege of choice. But to be in Diaspora is another type of uncertainty – it is memory and nostalgia, leaving a home when you're never really leaving. It is always explaining your existence, with less time to simply exist, or realise your existence in a way you fully get to choose.

I find myself always finding reasons to talk about Beirut, to tell the city's stories, our memories, to sit with it and care for it, joke with it and dance with it. We hate it. We also love it. I am unable to discern whether it is trauma contoured with memory, or memory with trauma. A trauma that causes us to unbutton in fragments, some of which are my own, firsthand, some inherited, and many a mutation of both.

To be an Arab-Muslim woman settler living on stolen land is to try to reassemble these fragments, to find meaning in them, to strive for a semblance of 'justice' and search for little joys and small loves in the disjoints of Diaspora.

ROOTS

For those of us who are accustomed to being one word, one step away from destruction, testimony is necessary. Memory is our best line of defence in a world that promises oblivion. Like fireflies, memories light up the different, dark corners of our lives and disappear. Sometimes, I cannot see them at all. I remain a world away, remembering things unremembered a world away – unable to participate fully in either world. Nostalgia is more than a reaction or romanticised notion or act of self-preservation. It is part of our heritage, but it is not permanent asylum, nor does it demand canonisation. It is a reservoir of insight, of empathy, it can bring our multitude of worlds closer.

Radical ways forward are rooted in tradition and nostalgia. As we learn more about ourselves, and where we cannot accept our present, we will refuse to resign ourselves to the same problems, the same scabs that flung us towards nostalgia in the first place.

SCRUB

Above all, nostalgia is not right or wrong – it merely is. And it is inescapable. Our present is a condition of it. We must reach a point where we are 'free' of our actual past – not free to forget it. Free to fight for something we know, to follow the blueprints, but not so focused that we can't make room for the unfamiliar. A room where we must make peace with the ever-expanding shadows, scrub its walls and cover them with wanderings and messes we have made, with shared pleasures, chaotic and delicate – signs that we are still breathing. A room that cannot be flattened. A room that does not deliver catharsis or resolution, redemption or equilibrium – just a refrain of returning, and beginning. Where there is no ending, only exits. A room that is ours. Where we, too, can sing – and sing home – in our own way.

Aunty has an answer for everything: idioms & other heirlooms

Qibla: how you face something matters

Men: there are men who keep taking the way the past does

Dreams: they'll clot like the blood between your legs

Lovers: whole only when someone else is inside

Friends: eventually, they all leave you behind – unless you leave first

Daughter: daughter/sister/mother/wife, your body is not yours but a trespassing

Choice: haunts you like a half-developed photograph that never fully pixelates

Failures: they go in for the kill. be careful not to drip a path back to your body

Arabic: you will spend your entire life trying to go home. keep this if you ever make it

Poison, you must pick one: sugarcane/maramiya/cardamom/tamarind/sharbat

Self: to find your kin, is to find your kind

Darling: Sara bint Saleh, the woman who takes her place in the world without permission is a dangerous thing.

There would be no jazz
after Safia

To my beloveds

my first heartbreak
for the night shift, fries were
cry as much as you need to
in the early years we slept
washed our feet
stayed up all night playing
sipped burnt chocolate
milky the way this place
kept spices in knotted plastic
zainab made the chutneys
thursday nights we crammed
with amar & yasir
on long weekends road

sara maria showed up
the order of the day
or we can sit here in silence
in each other's apartments
in each other's sinks
400 & d'n'ming
soup, made our coffee
taught us
blue bags the way our mothers did
& curries less chilli (for the weak)
into burwood's sheesha cafés
& mariam & mohammed
tripped to the blowhole, Wattamolla

the beaches of the south coast
battling over who can
parties with lins & aysh/es end in
we pledge allegiance to bush's playlist
heba will forever be my
we take two trains for a bite
& mehal & miran & shahd
of astute political analysis
of halal restaurant spreadsheets
as we forever lament our
& we ululated at the weddings
there for when
we lost family
said:

mariah on the radio
hit her high note (none of us)
limbs poking out of beds & bathtubs
& to the lyrics of 'no scrubs'
emergency contact
of banksia manoush at suhoor
patron saints of overthinking
of skincare routines
brunch is our religion
racist governments & misogynist community leaders
hated baby showers
all our grandmothers died in the same year
and we made one
every tv show we binged ever.

LIFE SENTENCE(S)

HELL

My first failure was the need to be seen.

Coal thinks the world is hot wherever you place it.

The thing they always notice
is I have my daddy's eyes.
I also have his charm and penchant for abuse.

To locate the ravenous self, 99 names I hold hostage.

To be inches away from ecstasy, but not there yet,
is the infinitely cruel moment of the journey.

I walk through this world unconsciously, in ghafla,
which is to say, most of my life I've been living in hell,
Ibn Arabi says, the people of hell are grateful.

How was he to know: seven days it took to destroy this body.

They charted my stars inconsolable, filled my womb with
quicksand – the only way to prevent trauma from passing down.

In this state of constant self-deification
I have been a slave to the animals inside me.

I begin the faithful work of burning.

HEAVEN

My first comfort was being seen.

Coal thinks the world is hot wherever you place it.
The world is covered in water.

The thing they always notice
is I have my daddy's eyes.
I also have his charm and penchant for patience.

To locate the one self, 99 names I embody.

To be on the edge of ecstasy, but not quite there yet,
is still ecstasy, an infinite moment of living hope.

I walk through this world consciously, in waking,
which is to say, most of my life I've been trying,
Ibn Arabi says, the people who praise are grateful.

He must have known: seven days it took to build this body.

They charted my stars noble, my womb a pilgrimage.
Trauma passes down – they never tell you healing
can be passed up.

In this state of constant self-deification
the station of being a slave to Allah ﷻ is freeing.

I begin the faithful work of liberation.

Aubade for the Alleyway
for T

Are we not stood here alone in the dead end
tucked behind the balconies of buildings and garbage skips
your farmer's hands hung on my hips, vulturous
your halo of charcoal curls damp in evening's breath
our distressed boots step synchronous
we make alchemy of the alleyway

if our mouths ever open, ever speak
if we crease the night with those words
we know our lives would be changed, forever
the stars in the Southern Cross a rebellion of embers,
and we, anchored in its eternal
phosphorescence in the alleyway

what business do we have with God
labouring in the fields of His worship
head tilted back in praise, every time the world
has killed me, I have learned to be grateful
death is good for everything except reason
if I touch you in this moment, all fear is abandoned in the alleyway

you kiss the rain from my mouth,
we are withered and mended by the crunch of
frosted autumn leaves and asphalt in the alleyway
if we are not supposed to dance, why all this music,
don't you hear it? We are in collective hum
with the universe of the alleyway

the moon of you moves into my shadow
an eclipse in the folds and frills of this alleyway
& like all things in rapture, what else can we do but drink
here, you, who I love, now and always, beyond this alleyway
dancing on rock in liminal space, we tear the skies
of our bodies, golden, in our alleyway

Love Poem to Consciousness

I have dreamt of Jenin and her groves,
the figs and orchards, almonds and apricots,
the olives that ripen and ricochet between fingers.

I have wedged and waded my palms
through the soil, marinating in its wetness
the rivers of olive oil spouting even in drought.

I have grazed the Central Highlands of al-Khalil
where the ravines roll and rise,
the terracotta terraces kiss the vineyards,
dark grape hyacinths panting,
the cicadas' wings glimmering like broken glass.

I have tracked down the oldest soap
factory in Nablus, one of two remaining,
a rush of milky rivers, batches of bars froth
into a foamy afternoon.

I have stepped onto the cobblestones
of al-Naserah, of prophecies and freshwater
spring, plumes of sacrament smoke
strangle the indigo dusk.

I have gazed at the crystalline waters of Akka,
felt the sting of salt puffy on my
lips, where I drank the undulating
ocean, and it drank me back.

I have traced the fishermen sailing out to
where the currents of east and west intersect, to
return with miscellany of red mullet and sea bass,
sequined and scaly. Protozoic offering, a beheading
for the fishmongers. I only discard the bones.

I have descended to the Jordan Valley,
breadbasket with no bread, shortage of water
for family and livestock, too emaciated to snip and
shear, farms and homes smothered by Caterpillars.

I have spent my years in deprivation,
nights uncertain if she was calling to me.

I know this now, my being contracts and expands
with the land, boundless.
I know this, too: if ancestral homeland
gets me killed someday,
I'll die like our trees, standing up.

Notes

Poems from this collection have appeared in the following books and magazines, some of them as earlier versions:

'little city' and 'Here, There: A Ghazal' appeared online in *bil 3arabi, Cordite Poetry Review*, 5 December 2019.

'Reading Darwish at Qalandia Checkpoint' was commissioned by the Australian Institute of Human Rights at UNSW for a book on gender justice and the international criminal court tentatively titled *Feminist Judgments: Re-imagining the International Criminal Court*, Cambridge University Press (forthcoming).

'Live from Gaza' appeared in *Rabbit: A Journal for Nonfiction Poetry*, Issue 34, *REPORTAGE*, 2022.

'The (Not So) Secret Life of 3arab Girls: Our Raqs Is Sharqi (An Intermittent Ghazal)' appeared in *Borderless: A transnational anthology of feminist poetry*, Recent Work Press, Canberra, 2021.

'Punctuation as Organised Violence' was exhibited at the Institute of Modern Art and appeared in *Meanjin*, Vol. 81, No. 4, Summer 2022.

'Border Control: Meditations' appeared in *Overland*, Issue 242, Autumn 2021.

'Elegy for a Body' appeared in *Admissions: Voices within Mental Health*, Upswell Publishing, 2022.

'Progressive (White Lover)' was commissioned by Red Room Poetry for Poetry Month 2023.

'The End of the World' appeared in *Speak*.

'The day home didn't change' appeared online in *Overland*, 4 August 2021.

—'broken ghazal for broken door' was inspired by Kafka's 'Before the Law' parable. In Arabic, the word 'bayt' denotes 'home', and it also means a line of poetry.

—'Aubade for the Ancestors': Mercurochrome is deliberately misspelled to reflect the way it was spoken.

—'The Year That Changed Everything': 'Israel' was called 'Milk and Honey' in a TV news report around the time of its foundation. 1948 is the year of the Nakba, and what Palestinians call the land known as 'Israel'. Eucalypts are non-native brought in by early Zionist settlers, and now proven poisonous to the land.

—'City/Sitti of Grief': 'Sitti' means 'Grandmother'.

—'Recipe for dinner and destruction': Twenty per cent of whatever I make from this book will go to Egna Legna, a collective of Ethiopian domestic workers based in Lebanon working to protect and preserve the dignity of the female domestic workers, and to abolish the kafala system.

—'Ode to Garbage (akh ya Libnen)': Research sources – https://www.theguardian.com/cities/2017/feb/02/beiruts-public-space-last-beach-residents-fear-privatisation-ramlet-al-baida. The last line of this poem is a Mahmoud Darwish derivative.

—'Reading Darwish at Qalandia Checkpoint': Cassius Turvey was a fifteen-year-old Noongar Yamatji boy, who was killed in a racist attack as he walked home from school with friends on 13 October 2022. Cassius's murder is emblematic of the deeply entrenched racism and anti-blackness of the Australian colony.

—'Live from Gaza': The poem's form of lists is inspired by M. NourbeSe Philip's *Zong!* #24. The concluding fade pays homage to Claudia Rankine's collection *Citizen*. The list of names of children killed in Israel's attack on Gaza in May 2021 is not exhaustive. There were dozens more Palestinians, including children, killed.

FLIRTY GIRLS

—'Kan ya Makan/Groppi': Powerhouse Egyptian belly dancer and actress Tahiya Carioca is said to have thrown her shoe at Hollywood darling Susan Hayward, who she overheard supposedly praising Israel for being a 'civilised nation' in the middle of an uncivilised region. American actor Danny Kaye got involved in defence of Hayward and was apparently also accidentally hit in the altercation.

—'Woman crying uncontrollably in the next stall responds': A response to the poem 'To the Woman Crying Uncontrollably in the Next Stall' by Kim Addonizio.

—'Stone': First line and form inspired by poet Franny Choi.

—'Ode to the WS train lines aka "Evil in the Suburbs"': Evil in the Suburbs is subversively used, speaking back to its oriental use in a book of the same title.

—'Bad Immigrant': Refers to the speech 'final solution' by then Australian Senator Fraser Anning.

—'Border Control: Meditations': The expression, *thanks God*, is common amongst immigrant families of 'Middle Eastern' background. I was first inspired to remember its usage by poet Kaveh Akbar.

—'There are no colonisers in this poem': The title is inspired by poet Teresa Dzieglewicz. Palestinian-American journalist Shireen Abu Akleh was killed by Israeli occupying forces while doing her job, reporting in the West Bank. According to the Committee to Protect Journalists, her death was not a tragic one-time event but actually part of a long, deadly pattern.

GIRLS WHO LIVE FOREVER

—'Thistle [to lose a ~~lover/country~~]': Title is inspired by poet George Abraham.

—'Eid 2016 (little and big)': With thanks to Steve Salaita.

—'Headlines': The line '*I really feel the mark of progress when I tick the check*' is after poet Ocean Vuong.

—'The End of the World': The stories of those who lost their lives in the Christchurch attack appear in this *Al Jazeera* article: https://www.aljazeera.com/news/2019/3/22/new-zealand-mosque-attack-who-were-the-victims.

—'Unholy Verses': First and foremost, Indigenous women who disproportionately feel the effects of climate change and the detrimental material effects of racial capitalism.

—'Lexicon': The poem is after poet Ocean Vuong. The line '*To speak properly you need to learn / the difference between free and three*' is borrowed from Eric Yip's *Fricataves*, a testament to our shared experiences learning languages not our own.

—'Ode to Teta's Building': 'Irrevocable condition' is a derivative of James Baldwin.

—'LIFE SENTENCE(S)': An infinite 'moment of living hope' is borrowed from Anne Carson.

—'Aubade for the Alleyway': The line '*if we are not supposed to dance, why all this music*' is borrowed from Gregory Orr.

AFTERLUDE

—'Love Poem to Consciousness': Jordan Valley is the lowest elevation point on earth. The line '*I'll die like our trees, standing up*' is after Mahmoud Darwish.

Acknowledgements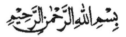

I start as I always do. With my utmost respect and reverence to the custodians of the land on which I live and write, Bidjigal land. I would also like to acknowledge with eternal gratitude Dharug land – parts of it known as Western Sydney – land that has sustained and grown me as an artist and activist. What a privilege, what a wonder, to be sharing stories on land where this has happened since time immemorial.

In Arabic, Bayt is a word for house and a line of poetry. So perhaps poetry is the ultimate place for the exiled. Thank you for the support to make these poems possible: Australia Council for the Arts, The Neilma Sidney Literary Travel Fund, The Myer Foundation and Writers Victoria, Red Room Poetry, Sweatshop Western Sydney, Writing NSW and Arab Theatre Studio. Thank you to the countless anthologies, literary journals and other platforms that have published my work: *Australian Poetry Journal*, *Australian Book Review*, *Cordite Poetry Review*, *Meanjin*, *Overland Literary Journal*, *Rabbit Poetry Journal* and *Speak*, amongst others. Thank you for making space for this poet. Thank you to the classrooms, community events, festivals and libraries for hosting me to speak and run workshops over the years.

Thank you to Aviva Tuffield for your warmth and for welcoming me to the UQP family, your (insurmountable!) faith and persistence seeing this collection through, your patience waiting for these poems to speak clearly. Thank you to the team at UQP for your care of these poems.

Thank you to poets Jeanine Leane, Nikky Finney, Hala Alyan and Alison Whittaker for responding when you did, how you did. Your words and work make me better.

I am eternally grateful to be in (poetry) community with you.

Thank you to Bella Li, keeper of poems, for your tender and rigorous mentorship, for helping me find structure and a sense of cohesion. Thank you Zainab Syed for the gift of your foresight and for halal:haram proofing this. Thank you to all members of my poetry family for nurturing me. Thank you to Bankstown Poetry Slam for creating and sustaining a community – and without whom I would not be as a poet. Thank you to the organisers and educators, particularly of the Palestine movement, without whom I would not be as a person.

Thank you to the women gathered around the coffee table, you have raised and nourished me for so long – from Beirut to Beverly Hills/Bidjigal Country and everything in between. I will carry your lessons with me wherever I go, and make sure everyone knows I stand on your shoulders.

Thank you to the (no)SATC, the guapas, brunch bishes, noodles, arab sisterhood, sobhiye network – you are all remarkable and I wouldn't be here without your friendship, wisdom, group chats and endless brunches.

Thank you to family, Salehs and Talebs, for loving me. To Mama and Baba, Ahmed, Omar and Aya. To my ancestors, I am so lucky to be part of this long line of words. I hope I have honoured you with this collection.

To Tarek: my forever home. Pancakes and ch … on Sundays.

Words are wayfarers and poems portals. I hope this collection transports and transforms you, dearest reader. Thank you.

I am so grateful for the privilege of publishing this collection, in a world that seeks to silence us and correct us and erase us. To adapt a line from the incomparable Nikky Finney: I have written the best I know how.